AFFIRMATIONS
from the
HEART
G *of* D

AFFIRMATIONS

from the

HEART

G*of*OD

Bridget Mary Meehan
and
Regina Madonna Oliver

Liguori
LIGUORI, MISSOURI

Library of Congress Cataloging-in-Publication Data

Meehan, Bridget.
  Affirmations from the heart of God / Bridget Mary Meehan
and Regina Madonna Oliver. — 1st ed.
      p.   cm.
    ISBN 0-7648-0172-4
        1. Self-esteem—Religious aspects—Christianity. 2.
Affirmations. I. Oliver, Regina Madonna, 1931– . II. Title.
BV4598.24.M44   1998
248.4—dc21   97–34250

Printed in the United States of America
02 01 00 99 98   5 4 3 2 1
First Edition

DEDICATION

To my parents, Jack and Bridie Meehan; Aunt Molly McCarthy; my brothers, Patrick and Sean; my sisters-in-law, Valerie and Nancy; and my niece and nephew, Katie and Danny.

—Bridget

To my parents, Harvey and Ethel Oliver; Aunt Fran Webster; my brother, David, and sister-in-law, Diane; my nieces and nephews, David Michael and Ellen Oliver, James Webster and Sylvia Ho Oliver, Barbara and Mark Forth, Carol Lee Oliver Tuohey, Laura Anne Forth, and William Webster Oliver; and my cousins, Eleanor Lamb, and Edy Jo and Melissa Southard.

—Regina

To our friends and mentors: Irene Marshall; Virginia Limon; Jutta, Christina and Alicia Clark; Sandra and Kevin Voelker; Francis Keefe; John Weyand; Joe Mulqueen; Eileen Dohn; Marcia and Barry Tibbits; Betty Wade; Susan Curcio; Patricia Byrne; Kathleen Bulger; Patricia McAleavy; Richard Sforza; Homer Sabatini; Andree Lanser; Daisy and Ogden Sullivan; Debbie Dubuque; Rosemary Walsh; Kathleen Wiesberg; Donna Mogan; Ellen and Cornelius Coakley; Luz and Rafael Sandiego; Douglas and Jojo Sandiego; Michal Morches; Maria and Steve Billick; Mary and Dick Guertin; Mary, Kevin, and Megan Fitzgibbons; Consilia Karli, Maureen Miele, Nancy Healy, and the Sisters for Christian Community; Susan and Gerald Gordon; Sara Muenster; Mary Trail; John Adams; Charlie Davis; Rea Howarth; Sister Rita McGarvey; Father Joseph McGarvey; Father Ron Falotico; Jerry Okoniewski; Father Mike Travaglione, OFM; Kay, David, and Tracey Welsh; Irene and John Walsh; Jim Brown; Bud Tyler; Pat Lehrer; Stella Melville; Doris and

Bob Schlesinger; Virgil and Darlene Spurlock; Alba and Lee Thompson; Marge and Dick Casey; Irene and Bill Manning; Marie McManus; Rev. and Mrs. Peter Reynierse; Gavina and Alexis King; Father Edward McCorkell, OCSO; Father Paul Wynants; Betty Turek; Sharon and Terry Danner; Peggy Gott; Ann Tennison; Eileen and Phil Thomas; Pat Zimmerman; Jim Webster; Jay and Kerri McDonald; Father Peter Phan; Charlie Hymers; Sister Mary Emma Hadrick (deceased); Sally Ann Nelson; Phyllis Kessinger; Phyllis and Wendell Hurst; Olga Gane; Carol and Ray Buchanan; Bob and Peg Bowen; Estelle Spachman; Father John Prinelli; Katherine Nee; Marge Weydert; Mary Horan; Grace Smith; and our various alma maters: The Graduate Theological Foundation of Donaldson, Indiana; Catholic University of America; Virginia Theological Seminary; Washington Theological Union; Marquette University; and Shalem Spiritual Institute, Washington, D.C.

To Anthony Chiffolo, editor at Liguori Publications, with gratitude.

CONTENTS

AFFIRMATIONS
from the
HEART
G *of* OD

PART I

STORIES
and
REFLECTIONS
about
AFFIRMING LOVE

STORIES AND REFLECTIONS ABOUT AFFIRMING LOVE

Regina's Story

Frances Webster, my aunt, was in the habit of talking to herself. Sometimes her mumblings would reach an audible volume, and someone in the family would hear her spit out at her image in the mirror: "You are so stupid! Just so stupid!" She would enunciate each syllable with a venom that made the family wonder if she really thought that badly of herself. This was a concern to everyone because Fran was an incredibly wonderful human being—one of the most self-sacrificing people we had ever known. She never had harsh things to say of anyone else—only of herself. But since the recital of negative self-evaluations was habitual for her, we had to wonder how many times during her ninety-two years she had flung maledictions at herself. What impact would this kind of assault have had on her subconscious? And on her spiritual life, her relationship with God? We all found her wonderfully lovable, so why couldn't she understand that God did too?

Bridget's Story

Molly McCarthy, my aunt, was an equally incredible human being, but she was amazingly affirmative throughout her life in all circumstances. She seemed to be serenely positive in her interchanges with others and greatly at peace with her own self-worth. Molly would always say, "That's all right, dear. Things will work out all right!" She thought of everyone, including herself, as God-loved and, therefore, as good!

Bridget and Regina's Reflections

These two aunts, although of quite different backgrounds, were quite fond of each other and got along famously. Now that they are both with God, we wonder if Aunt Fran has reached the bliss of knowing what Aunt Molly already knew—that God loves her enormously.

By telling real-life stories, this book will show that we all sometimes tend to see life, ourselves, and others in ways that Love does not intend. Here is the beauty of the Resurrection message: God, who is totally positive, affirming Love, can transform even the worst! And no Christian has any business wallowing in negatives! After all, our Creator God called *all* of creation "very good."

This book will also offer some prayer therapies to cure us of any negative thinking that may have crept into our subconscious, because from there it can surreptitiously poison our outlook on ourselves, deaden our hopes for the future, and stunt our ability to dream noble dreams and aspire to great heights. Negative thinking can spiritually bleed us to death, like a giant ulcer, without our even knowing what is wrong. For how many people who say, "I'm depressed!" is the real problem their struggle against a lifelong influx of negative self-abuse?

Regina's Story

But "How dare we!" I heard a spiritual director once say. "How dare we speak badly of one whom God made and called 'Good'!" So we offer some models of affirming prayer, which we believe are attuned to God's original heart-response to the miracle of creatures newly formed. The heart of God formed the word of God about the newborn creation of which each person is the epitome: "Good! Very Good!"

Bridget's Story

Susan, a vibrant, middle-aged woman, broke into tears as she sat in my office sharing her story. She blamed herself for the difficulties in her marriage. "I am fat, ugly, and undeserving of love, trapped in a relationship going nowhere," she reflected.

After several sessions of prayer for healing of her negative self-image, during the final meeting Susan was upbeat: "When I opened myself to God's unconditional love, I was able to appreciate my good qualities for the first time, like my sense of humor. Now I see myself as deserving love and giving love. On my bathroom mirror I put a sign that reads, 'I am a beautiful image of my God.' I begin my day by looking into the mirror and repeating this message. Some mornings I even sing it as I shower. Once in a while my husband joins me. I know we have a long way to go, but I am more hopeful. It feels good to have fun together again."

Bridget and Regina's Reflections

Like Aunt Fran, many of us have absorbed negative input about ourselves over the entire course of our lives. We may have been asked, "Why are you so stupid?" or "Why can't you be like your brother or sister?" or we may have been told, "You'll never amount to anything!" Such hurtful utterances damage our self-esteem on a level we can't even imagine. We even say these things to ourselves, as a kind of daily negative litany.

Bridget's Story

In the fifties my family, the Meehans from Coolkerry, County Laois, Ireland, emigrated to the United States. I still remember my first year at St. Thomas More School in Arlington, Virginia. I was a chubby little girl with curly hair. At recess, some of my classmates would tease me about the way I talked. Some called me "fatso" and would not let me join in their games. I often cried, couldn't concentrate in school, and felt as if I didn't belong. My schoolwork suffered as a result as well. To make matters worse, that year our nun became ill after the first month of school, and we had a number of substitute teachers who did not speak English.

I did not begin to flourish in my new environment until the fourth grade, when a lovely, gentle nun, Sister Marita Louise, expressed her belief in me. She would stop by my desk and praise my efforts. I could tell from the sparkle in her eye that she liked my Irish brogue. My spirit soared, my grades improved, and I made new friends. Affirmations always build us up.

Sometimes, we will not have a Sister Marita Louise to affirm us, and we will then need to do something ourselves to overcome the negative messages that we repeat to ourselves or that others repeat to us. Replacing "You're not good enough!" "You're not smart enough!" "Don't even try that!" "You're too young!" "You're too old!" "Nobody wants to hear your opinion!" "Go away, and don't come back!" with positive, life-giving messages such as "I love and accept myself just the way I am!" "God wants me to do great things!" and "I choose to experience the divinity within" can completely transform our self-perceptions. Speaking such truthful, gentle messages of love to ourselves can nourish our spirits and open us to the Holy Spirit speaking in the depths of our souls. When we repeat affirmations like these, we are hearing God speak to us, and we come to understand that God's love for us is beyond our imagining. We become aware of a whole new joyful way of living. Once we have known this kind of wondrous love, we will never be the same. Our lives will be an expression of Divine Love.

Our family has remained in close contact with relatives in Ireland, exchanging letters and phone calls almost monthly. I will never forget our many trips to our homeland. Each time we landed at Shannon Airport, relatives would greet us with big smiles and warm hugs. Usually, we'd spend a week or two visiting cousins in County Laois. Sometimes they would join us on excursions around the Emerald Isle. Together we'd explore this beautiful land with its silvery-blue lakes, purple-heathered bogs, sheep-dotted mountains, and deserted sandy beaches.

Twenty years ago our family was having a great time in Ballyheigue, a scenic town on the western coast of Ireland. On one windy summer's evening, when everyone else was at tea, I took a walk by myself. I was feeling anxious about a major change in my life. As I strolled along the ocean's edge, the majestic waves were breaking at my feet, the salt air blowing through my hair. Clouds, like angels, danced across the sky, and a rosy sun painted the horizon crimson. I felt a peace descending on me. In the depths of my soul I heard God assuring me, "I will love you forever with all my love." At that moment I knew that no matter what happened, all would be well. It was, and is to this day, one of the most powerful spiritual experiences of my life.

Visiting or reminiscing about the places that have been significant in our lives is often helpful and affirming. Some people make a "spiritual" pilgrimage to the houses that have been home for them in the past. I made such a visit to the three-room cottage where I and my two brothers, Patrick and Sean, spent our earliest years together with our grandfather Papa Beale. I walked to the spring where we drew water from the well. Then I went to Grogan, to the church, now boarded up, where Mom and Dad were married fifty years ago. I sat in the church in Rathdowney where I made my first holy Communion, right under the stained-glass window of St. Bridget. I stopped at Lady's Well, where Dad's band would play every year on the feast of the Assumption, and from where we always carried home bottles of blessed water. My last stop was the cemetery at Ballyroan, to place my hand on the tombstone of Grandfather and Grandmother Meehan. This kind of journey affirms our very existence by putting us in touch with our roots. We see that the ordinary things in life are spiritual, and the spiritual is ordinary because every breath of life is grace-laden.

As we tune into Divine Wisdom dwelling in our hearts, we often find thoughts and insights that have the power to heal and transform our lives. Maria, a young, single mother, was worried that bad things would happen to her baby. Then one night after tucking in her infant and kissing him good night, she closed her eyes and prayed a blessing over him. As she prayed, she saw an image of the Blessed Mother holding her baby and herself close to her breast. Reflecting on this comforting image, Maria realized that God loved her baby more than she or any human parent could. The image of Mary continues to calm Maria. "No matter how hard it is," she reflects, "I know we are not alone; my child and I are held in God's embrace."

Bridget and Regina's Reflections

God's message of affirming love can come to us in many forms. Some people might see an image. Others might receive the message when a friend places a hand on our shoulder and reminds us that we are special, saying, "You are intelligent and strong" or "I thank God for your smile." John, who was recovering from an addiction, once shared what happened when friends in a twelve-step program challenged him to "discover God's goodness within": "It changed my life. I no longer saw myself as a miserable, worthless human being. God's amazing grace helped me find inner treasures that had been truly lost. I felt like a new person. It was like a ton of bricks had fallen from my shoulders, and I knew serenity for the first time in my life."

Another of the ways we can discover God's affirming love is by repeating positive messages that we have "heard" God speak to us in the depths of our souls. Two inspiring mantras are "God is loving me now" and "God is loving *through* me now." One can repeat them often during the day. These affirmations help us realize that God is closer to us than the next breath, and that we can be divine instruments of love in our encounters with other people.

As we go about our routine activities, such as waiting in line at the store, driving around in the car, or doing household chores, the repetition of one of these affirmations renews our confidence in the divine abundance of God's Spirit that is always with us and in us. We really need this all the time, but especially when we are tired, impatient, and burned out.

You can discover an affirming mantra of your own. Think for a moment of a name that you would like to call God today, and file it in your memory for a minute. Think of an affirming statement that feels right for you today. Put the two together. Now you have your mantra for the day. You can use this in the same way that some of us were taught to use aspirations in Catholic school or CCD. You simply repeat your mantra over and over whenever you think of it during the day.

God is within us. This is basic scriptural theology right from the lips of Christ: "Live on in me, as I do in you" (John 15:4). Isn't it amazing that this message comes to us as a surprise?

Bridget's Story

Caring for my frail eighty-five-year-old mother is helping me realize how very fragile life is, and how important it is to see every moment as a gift. Dad and I pray that God will love Mom through us. Watching her weaken and slip away day by day is painful. Mom prays her rosary daily, no matter how she is feeling. Often, I sit nearby just to be in her presence. When I look into her eyes, she sometimes seems so far away. It's almost as if a veil is slowly rising, and Mom is stepping gently into another world. I believe God is giving her a sneak preview of the magnificent things to come in the heavenly realm. Throughout her life, Mom has welcomed God however, whenever, wherever, and in whomever God comes, and now she is discovering God's closeness in sickness, dependence, and old age. As many people can affirm, God speaks to us through suffering, tears, and losses. In recent years, I have been learning much about love that lasts forever by listening to God speak to me through my mother's eyes.

My mother reminds me that I am getting older too. Here I am a middle-aged baby boomer. Menopause is fast approaching, coming like a thief in the night to steal me away to some dark place I don't want to go.

But I am resisting. Sure, my hair is graying. No problem, I can color it. My weight is shifting; no problem, I diet and exercise. Then there are the wrinkles. I wonder what beauty cream will be my fountain of youth this month. What am I going to do about those hormonal changes? Sometimes, I don't know whether to laugh or cry! So I moan and groan a little. Part of me realizes that I am dealing with the death of my youth. And part of me feels grateful to be alive, healthy, and enthusiastic about life. I appreciate the gifts of every passing moment that I took for granted for so long: a golden ray of sunlight gilding the kitchen table where we sit for our morning tea, the perfume of daffodils in our garden filling me with a sense of spring and hope, the taste of fresh Irish scones baking in the oven—the small, everyday things that I was too busy to notice before. I have time now to savor the treasures that are right now, right here in front of me. All these little things are gifts from the infinite, loving God to me.

And all the little things in your life that you may have allowed to go unnoticed are gifts from the infinite loving God to *you!*

Bridget and Regina's Reflections

Open your eyes and look around you. What can you see? hear? taste? touch? smell? What brings you joy?

comfort? strength? peace? No matter what passage or stage of life you are in, God is with you, loving you. Why not saturate yourself with this realization by praying a litany of thanks at the beginning and end of each day, naming all the little things that now have become big things for you because you see them as God's personal gifts?

Nothing can separate you from God's love for you. God loves you more than any person ever could. The story is told of Teresa of Ávila that in prayer she heard God say, "Teresa, if I had never made the world, I would have made it for you." God is saying the same thing to you: "Mary, Frances, Irene, Lucy, Frank, Joe, Sean, Patrick, _____, if I had never made the world, I would make it just for you."

Even if you are feeling down or blue, all you have to do to encounter the Love of your life is open yourself up to God, who like a mother reaches out to comfort you. Jesus reminded us of the nurturing tenderness in the heart of our God: "Oh, how often have I yearned to gather you together, like a hen gathering her chicks under her wings…" (Matthew 23:37). Have you ever realized that God has been mothering you all your life, and continues to do so? You can call on God's mothering nature whenever you need it, just as you called your mother whenever you needed her.

Call out, crying your need, and expect a loving response.

God loves you through everyone who loves you. Think of all those people who have touched you lovingly during your life: the doctor who assisted at your birth; the nurse who tucked you into your mother's arms; the daddy who stood by through the whole process and welcomed you with a smile of delight as he tucked your baby fingers around his outstretched hands and marveled at the perfection of so small a creature; the mother who suckled you, bathed you, changed your diapers, caressed you; brothers and sisters, so much a part of your growth at every moment; playmates and later school friends who shared your childhood secrets; teachers whose infinite patience taught you the rudiments of all you know today; and so on through all those who touched your life any time along the way. Think of all these, one by one. Now you have a litany of the people who blessed your life, and you can call on God to bless theirs.

Listening to God's affirming love challenges us to cradle others and shoulder their burdens with a compassionate heart. Sometimes this is easy to do, but other times not. When we are tired or impatient, we may not have the energy to concentrate on another's needs, but a simple breath prayer such as "The Spirit of God fills me" (as you breathe in) and "I breathe forth the Spirit of God to touch the life of _____ " (as you breathe out) can be a simple but effective way of touching another's life. When we are more recollected and at peace ourselves, we can "pray" for others by allowing divine warmth, kindness, and solace to flow through us to all those crying out to us for love. Sometimes we do this by simply listening to another person and affirming the preciousness of that person's being. Being a loving presence for others will lift their spirits and heal their souls.

God's affirming love enables us to be beacons of love for our family, friends, and close associates, but it also reveals that God is calling us to be channels of divine peace, love, and justice in the world at large. Often this can be difficult, for it can mean putting our time, energy, money, reputation, even life on the line to help those in need. It can also mean pitching in to transform structures that discriminate and oppress people. Listening to God's affirming love can wake us up to recognize God's love for everyone, especially the marginalized and dispossessed people in our society. Love can enable us to assist communities or groups, such as the Catholic Worker, Network, and Bread for the World, in their activities for peace and justice. Joining with others to live God's reign in our time, we celebrate our human solidarity, our human worth and wonderfulness, our value before God.

God wants us to internalize the divine value system, so contradictory to the world's. Our God has "deposed the mighty from their thrones and raised the lowly to high places," has "filled the hungry with good things" and "sent the rich away empty" (Luke 1:52–53). God values each one of us immeasurably, no matter how other people may calculate our worth, and wants us to love and cherish even those rejected and despised by society. As Jesus taught us, "The truth is, every time you did this for the least of my sisters or brothers, you did it for me" (Matthew 25:40). The bottom line: loving our neighbor *is* loving God.

Living in God's affirming love means living a life of love and service. It means doing all we can to bring harmony and peace to the world. Each day, we can bring heaven to earth in all we think, say, and do, and we will be judged, according to Jesus, on how well we sow God's love throughout the world.

How can we enlarge the reign of God when our own and others' selfishness too often get in the way of our best intentions? We can love, because God has first loved us. God believes in us and empowers us with a passionate Spirit to do even greater things than we could possibly imagine. We do not have to wait until we are perfect. If we did, we would be waiting until "one minute after our eternity begins!" We simply need to be open to God's healing action within ourselves and, simultaneously, to follow as the Spirit prompts us to intercede and act on behalf of others. As Jesus assured us, "The truth of the matter is, anyone who has faith in me will do the works I do—and *greater* works besides" (John 14:12; emphasis added). This is our scriptural affirmation from the very heart of God.

So when people argue that affirming prayer is a very limited form of prayer because "I have so many things wrong with me that if I went about it this way I might not even make it before my deathbed!" we must answer, "Yes—if it all depends on us." But the good news is: it doesn't depend on us! At least not on us alone. It depends on the ever-present God *within* us who is always working in every situation, relationship, and event of our lives. Prayer is answered! In ways that surpass our greatest expectations! In God's affirming love, *all things are possible!* All we have to do is open our hearts to our affirming God.

PART II

EIGHT
METHODS
of
PRAYING
AFFIRMATIONS

1

"THE DAILY DOSE"

Here are five affirmations for everyone to use every-day at the beginning of prayer time. This way you begin your day on a prayerful, positive note. These aspirations/mantras can heal, liberate, and empower you on your spiritual journey.

I affirm that I am a beautiful creation of my birthing God!

I affirm that I am in process; God is continuing to form me into the vision God has of me!

I affirm that I love God, that I love God's vision for me, and that I love God's vision for the whole created universe!

I affirm that I love others, my neighbors—both those who do me good and those who injure me, those I know personally, and those I have never met—and I pray for their healing and wholeness.

I see myself, those I love, and all creation as already whole and healed in the heart of God. This day I will think and act as if this vision is already a reality.

2

THE ACCEPTANCE
OF OUR LOVE-NAME

You may have a favorite name for God on any given
day that is especially expressive of your relationship
at that time. Sometimes we may want to call God
"Abba" (Daddy). Sometimes we might call God
"Ammah" (Mommy). We may want to call God by a
scriptural title: "Shaddai" (the one who satisfies every need) or "Emmanuel" (God-with-us). Or we may
want to say, "My Heart" or "My Love" or "My Everything." Have you ever realized that God has a love-
name for you? God does, of course, since God is
author of this natural tendency of ours to give nick-
names or love-names to others.

Would you like to know the love-name God has for
you? Here is a prayer exercise to help you discover
what it is. Of course, it requires a leap of faith. You
will be tempted to say to yourself, "I just made that
up!" But reflect on this: God is so completely
"Emmanuel"—God-with-us—that you are in God and
God is in you just as the fish is in the ocean and the

ocean is in the fish. The fish does not realize this because this "being in" is so much an every-moment, every-day experience that it is taken for granted. It is simply "the way of things" in the life of a fish. Just so, our being in God and God's being in us is "the way of things" in our lives and, therefore, is hardly perceived as amazing and wonderful—or, as children say, "awesome!"

God's way of naming people in Scripture always indicates something of the wonderful plan God has for that person. God challenges us in name-giving to become what the name means. Jesus challenged Simon to *become* "rock" in naming him "Peter."

To discover the love-name God has for you,

Sit in a comfortable place, and take with you a tablet, pen, and your Bible. Read the story of Peter's calling in John 1:35–42.

Tell Jesus you know God has great plans for you, and you would like to know the love-name God has in mind, the name that challenges you to become what God envisions for you. Then say, "When you think of me, Jesus, what gift of grace do you see in me that you treasure?"

On your paper write the title "Gifts of Grace."

✍

Write: You are _____, and fill in the blank with the grace-gift that comes to mind. (It might read, "kind to the elderly and helpless" if that is one of your gifts, "a bearer of good news" if you are one who finds occasions to compliment the accomplishments of others, or "a wise counselor" if people always seem to come to you for advice.)

✍

Ask the question in #2 two more times, and write down your responses. Now you have identified three grace-gifts.

✍

Read these over. Are they true of you? Would you willingly give away any one of these affirmations? (Not if they ring true. The realization that God is affirming you will be too dear!)

✍

Read them over again and ask Jesus, "Dear Lord, is there a word, a name, that summarizes these things you say of me? Help me discover the love-name you have for me."

The word or name may come to you easily, flashing across your mind. Or it may come later, when you pick up your Bible, or as you wake from sleep tomorrow. Or a friend may say to you: "I think God would call you _____." Don't be obsessive about this. When the word comes to you, you will recognize it as true and challenging.

When you have the word that is your love-name, write it on the page with your three affirmations. If it is really meaningful to you, you may want to print it out in calligraphy from your computer and frame it; or you may want to embroider it, or create a keepsake in some other significant way. Revelation 2:17 shows God giving to "the one who overcomes...a white stone—a stone with a new name written on it, known only to the person who receives it." To make a simple memento, find a small, smooth, white stone and write your love-name on it. Regina has such a stone at home that she has kept for many years, and on it is the word *Shama,* about which she asked God and heard the word *Listener!* She often reflects on this name and wishes to be a better "listener" to God's plan for her. During Lent this year, Regina read a commentary explaining that the word *listen* in Hebrew had the significance of "obey." This gave her much to think about regarding her sometimes not-so-ready response to God.

Thank God for your name, and continue to be aware of its significance for your life.

3

THE HEALING TOUCH OF JESUS: A PRAYER EXPERIENCE FOR INNER HEALING

Begin this prayer time by playing soft, instrumental music....

*

Take time to be still....

*

Breathe slowly in through your nose and out through your mouth for a couple of minutes until you feel calm....

*

As you inhale, breathe in the healing power of God....

*

As you breathe out, breathe out any darkness or block-age that keeps you from experiencing God's love for you....

✍

Repeat one of the following words to help you center: *Jesus, Savior, Healer, Friend....*

✍

If you become distracted, simply let go of the distrac-tion, and continue to repeat your prayer word....

✍

Simply be in the presence of the Holy One....

✍

Open yourself to amazing grace....

✍

Imagine yourself walking along the ocean. The sky is clear and blue. The wind is blowing gently. Seagulls are flying above the sparkling, dancing waters. You marvel at the beauty of God's creation all around you....

✍

You see some tall grass nearby. You can hear the rustle of the grass....

✍

You decide to sit down. You close your eyes and gently drop off to sleep....

✍

Someone is moving toward you. You recognize Jesus. He sits beside you. He embraces you and reveals his heart for you. "I love you tenderly, boundlessly, completely. You are my beloved, my heart's delight. Let nothing separate you from me ever. I am always with you."

✍

You talk with Jesus about a particular weakness, situation, or relationship in which you need help. You pour out all your feelings, hurt, frustration and pain....

✍

Jesus listens and looks into your eyes with a love that fills you. He places his hands on your head and gently holds them there....

You feel a power coming from those outstretched hands filling you with warmth, relief, and release....

You know Jesus is healing you somewhere deep inside....

You are filled with thanksgiving, joy, love! You put all of this into the words "Thank you, Jesus, thank you, Jesus...."

You enjoy the presence of Jesus and come gently back to the awareness of the people and situation around you....

You can repeat this experience whenever you experience the need of Jesus' healing touch.

※

You can become aware that God is always with you every moment of every day.

※

You can enter deeply into the heart of God.

4

AFFIRMATIONS FROM THE HEART OF GOD

Listen to the following affirmations that reflect God's love for you. Repeat one that touches you as you go about your daily activities throughout the day. Or make up one of your own especially suited to your needs.

(your name), I am your deepest joy/peace/hope.

✽

(your name), I love you with all my love.

✽

(your name), I am your comfort in cares and sorrows.

✽

(your name), I am your heart's delight.

✽

(your name), I am your deepest longing.

※

(your name), I am the love of your life.

※

(your name), I rejoice over you this day.

※

(your name), I thought of you before you were conceived; I gave birth to you.

※

(your name), I delight in you.

※

(your name), I glory in your gifts.

※

(your name), I forgive and heal you.

※

(your name), I strengthen you.

※

(your name), I give you my peace.

☙

(your name), if I had never made the world I would make it just for you!

☙

(your name), I am in you; you are in me!

☙

(your name), I am with you always.

☙

(your name), I give you the greatest gift, my Spirit.

☙

(your name), I give you boundless joy, passionate love, and amazing abundance.

☙

(your name), I see you as my perfect reflection.

Image God looking directly into your eyes and saying the following:

(your name), in my heart I embrace you.

(your name), in my wounds I heal you.

(your name), in my arms I lift you up.

(your name), discover divinity within you.

(your name), I love you.

(your name), I walk with you.

(your name), I bless you and nurture you.

(your name), I live in your heart.

≫

(your name), open yourself to my healing.

≫

(your name), let my strength fill you.

≫

(your name), let my peace surround you.

≫

(your name), my wisdom will direct you.

≫

(your name), I will take infinitely better care of (name of person) than you can ever imagine.

≫

(your name), walk with me.

≫

(your name), talk with me.

≫

(your name), your body is one of my favorite dwelling places.

☙

(your name), I give you my heart.

☙

(your name), be with me.

5

AFFIRMATIONS
FROM SCRIPTURE

(your name), "I have called you by name, you are mine" (Isaiah 43:1; NRSV).

(your name), "you are precious in my sight, and honored, and I love you" (Isaiah 43:4; NRSV).

(your name), "when you pass through the waters, I will be with you; and through the rivers, they shall not overwhelm you" (Isaiah 43:2; NRSV).

(your name), "when you walk through fire you shall not be burned, and the flame shall not consume you" (Isaiah 43:2; NRSV).

(your name), "your God…will rejoice over you with gladness" (Zephaniah 3:17; NRSV).

(your name), "I will bring you home" (Zephaniah 3:20; NRSV).

(your name), "as a mother comforts her child, so I will comfort you" (Isaiah 66:13; NRSV).

(your name), "your grief will turn to joy" (John 16:20).

(your name), "as my Abba has loved me, so have I loved you" (John 15:9).

(your name), "I will be your parent, and you will be my child" (Hebrews 1:5).

※

(your name), "live on in my love" (John 15:9).

※

(your name), "live on in me, as I do in you" (John 15:4).

※

(your name), "it was not you who chose me; it was I who chose you to go forth and bear fruit…" (John 15:16).

※

(your name), "ask, and you will receive so that your joy will be complete" (John 16:24).

※

(your name), "you will suffer in the world. But take courage! I have overcome the world" (John 16:33).

※

(your name), "anyone who has faith in me will do the works I do—and greater works besides" (John 14:12).

(your name), "don't let your hearts be distressed; don't be fearful" (John 14:27).

(your name), "peace I leave with you; my peace I give to you" (John 14:27).

(your name), "your faith has saved you. Go in peace" (Luke 7:50).

(your name), "rejoice and be glad: your reward will be great in heaven" (Luke 6:23).

6

PRAYER THERAPY
FOR HEALING LIFE'S HURTS

Find a few minutes for this prayer therapy and a quiet
place to be with the Divine Therapist.

Choose an area in your life in which you need
to experience God's love: for example, a situation or relationship in your life that needs
transforming, grief for the loss of a loved one,
a resentment toward a specific person with all
the emotional baggage that is attached to it, an
addiction that has seemed impossible to break,
a stress situation at work that will not go away,
a call to service.

Step into Divine Wisdom and open yourself to
the changes that God would like to bring to
your life. Notice how different your life could
be if this loss, relationship, addiction, stress,
or service is transformed in this way. Then, in-

vite Wisdom to open you to God's love in this situation.

Write down a positive statement that expresses God as comforting, healing, empowering, or doing what you most need God to do for you or through you right now. Some examples are "I experience God's strength in me," "I let go of my fear, doubt, or loss and let God fill me with peace," "God, replace my need for alcohol/sex/food (or whatever else) with an awareness of your infinite love," or "God's love flows through me to (name of a person or group)."

Repeat your affirmation often. Put written copies of your affirmation in places that will help you remember to repeat it. Repeating affirmations helps you "act as if" the positive belief or thought you desire is already a reality. For example, when you repeat the words "I experience God's strength in me," you become filled with an awareness of God's strength permeating your whole being. When you affirm that

God is filling you with love, you experience this love transforming every aspect of your life.

7

PRAYER THERAPY
FOR AFFIRMING OTHERS

As members of God's family, we are all interconnected. Every thought and word we experience has the power to bless and heal another person. The following prayer provides words that can heal and transform our relationships. Imagine yourself affirming others in your prayers each day: your family, friends, coworkers, boss, neighbors, faith community, and so on.

Open yourself to the love in the heart of God for them.

Imagine yourself looking into their eyes and saying one or more of the following affirmations:

(person's name), I love you.

(person's name), you are a special gift in my life.

(person's name), your smile brightens my day.

🖋

(person's name), your goodness (kindness, generosity, sincerity…) touches me.

🖋

(person's name), you are a bright sunbeam of God's love.

🖋

(person's name), your work makes a difference to me.

🖋

(person's name), I appreciate your presence.

🖋

(person's name), you inspire (help, strengthen, support,…) me.

🖋

(person's name), you are creative (responsible, dependable, competent,…).

🖋

(person's name), you are a wonderful friend.

(person's name), you have a great sense of humor.

(person's name), I give thanks to God for you.

(person's name), I trust you completely.

(person's name), the more I get to know you, the more I love you.

(person's name), you are so much fun.

You can also create your own affirmations for the special people in your life.

As a fruit of your praying, you may be drawn to speak aloud this affirmation or compliment the next time you meet these people.

You may be led to telephone someone right now, to express your love and appreciation for her or him.

8

PRAYER THERAPY
FOR AFFIRMING
THE GOODNESS OF CREATION

As we approach the twenty-first century, we are more aware than ever of our cosmic citizenship, the sacredness of the earth and the vastness of the universe. As members of a global village, we can respond to the Spirit's invitation to experience the marvels of God's wondrous love in our lives everywhere we turn in the world. Open yourself to the love in the heart of God for self and creation.

Imagine yourself looking into a mirror or at God's creation and saying one or more of the following affirmations:

I am joyous, free, and serene.

*

I am uplifted by the creative Spirit of God.

*

O God of living waters, saturate my heart.

🖋

Like the stars at night, I am robed in your luminous light.

🖋

I see your holiness shining in nature's colors.

🖋

I see miracles all around me.

🖋

God of all creation, I awaken to earth's gifts.

🖋

Divine Beloved, the earth is my home and your home.

🖋

Today I unite myself with all people on planet Earth.

🖋

I bless God for the harmony I experience with the sun, moon, and stars.

🖋

I dance for joy with the flowers, plants, and trees.

🖋

I taste with delight earth's abundance.

🖋

I play with you in the spring rain (autumn breeze, summer sunshine, winter frost).

🖋

All creatures great and small remind me of the Playful Creator.

🖋

This day I will dance with gratitude for the wonder of clouds, sky, birds, and animals.

🖋

How marvelous, O Divine Beloved, is the universe you created.

🖋

Blessed are you, eternal Source of the cosmos.

Ⓦ

I live in a magnificent world that nurtures me.

Ⓦ

Love divine, you are the breath of every living thing.

Ⓦ

Gracious One, you are all around me.

Ⓦ

I praise God for my pet, _____, whom I cherish.

Ⓦ

All the earth is holy ground.

You can also create your own affirmations for the special places and creatures in your life.

PART III

QUESTIONS
for
INDIVIDUAL
REFLECTION
and
GROUP
DISCUSSION

QUESTIONS FOR INDIVIDUAL REFLECTION AND GROUP DISCUSSION

When you become aware of your negative thoughts and beliefs, you can choose to release them and replace them with positive, healing words. You may want to get together with a friend, counselor, or spiritual director to share your journey to spiritual transformation. You may want to get together with a supportive community who are using affirmations. You may want to reflect on your own growth in a journal. These questions are offered to stimulate reflection and sharing in one or more of these situations.

How can prayerful affirmations help us to experience God's transforming love?

What impact can affirmations have on our spiritual growth?

꿔

In what ways can affirmations free and heal us?

꿔

How can affirmations help us to develop stronger relationships with significant others in our lives?

꿔

Can the use of affirmations be a positive power in effecting greater world harmony?

꿔

How can affirmations help to heal divisions in the Church?

꿔

Have affirmations changed my image(s) of God?

꿔

Have affirmations affected my relationship with God? In what way(s)?

How would I characterize my relationship with God now, and what direction does it seem to be taking as a result of my use of affirmations?

How does this practice affect my self-image and my potential to heal myself? My view of others and my potential to help them? My view of creation and my potential to heal the earth?

What effect does filling my mind with positive and healing thoughts have on my attitudes and behaviors?

Do I agree with the saying "As people think, so they are"? How can affirmations change the way I think and perceive life? How can affirmations help me to grow in wholeness and holiness?

PART IV

CONCLUSION

CONCLUSION

A word of caution to all who begin to work with affirming prayers: pick and choose from the various possibilities offered one or two that particularly appeal to you, and be faithful to using them at least *twice daily* during the time you set aside for prayer. You can choose to use them at other times, if you wish—for example, when you take a "prayer break" instead of a "coffee break"—and you should find yourself refreshed. But anyone who, in a "gung-ho" mood for the novelty of a newfound prayer-toy, tries to do several different styles at once is likely to come down with spiritual indigestion. The many suggestions offered are varied to allow the reader a *choice* and to furnish the pray-er a variety that should serve for many years.

The Holy Spirit is always at work in us interiorly, bringing us gently and piecemeal toward total integration (and that is what *holiness* is—the integration and maturity achieved by God's freeing and healing action at the core of our being). And God's Holy Spirit will act on our ailing souls to heal the most obvious spiritual frailty first. That is why you may feel drawn to use a particular type of affirmation exercise. You, on the subconscious level, and God both know your most painful weakness, the one that God intends to heal *now!* So you will be led to choose the affirmation that is best for your prayer therapy now, at this time. As the affirmation begins to soothe and penetrate the hurting spot, you will know it is working because of the relief you experience—whether you can name the hurt or not. You may then become aware of a desire to use a different form of affirmation. Never be afraid to "go where the Spirit leads"!

When beginning the pursuit of spiritual maturity or holiness by allowing God to *act* on the point of their greatest trauma, some people have found it helpful to confide in another person, who serves as a spiritual friend. Others find a spiritual journal helpful, writing down their prayer experiences, hopes, confusions, anticipations, and so on in a diary style that is a written dialogue between the person and God. One advantage of sharing our spiritual journey in these ways is the greater emphasis we are thus giving to our spiritual life, as well as the feedback that can serve as a "reality check."

Why is the use of affirmations important for you,

and how will it help you to become a holy and whole person? Let's admit that the negative, debilitating harangue that plays and replays in our heads triggers all kinds of unhealthy defenses in us, and that all of us suffer, more or less, from a lifetime of bombardment from such verbal abuse.

Let's also admit, as much as we may hate to, that all of us are "broken wings." We are so very far from the wonderful dream in the heart of our Creating God who made us and who knows our potential. We do not understand why this is so, but we *do* experience it as true—and we know ourselves to be imperfect. Our inability to be our true selves is what has been referred to as original sin. But God who is goodness is bent upon reuniting us with our true selves and bringing us to *wholeness,* which is the same as *holiness.* As St. Paul assures us, "Eye has not seen, ear has not heard, nor has it so much as dawned on anyone what God has prepared for those who love God" (1 Corinthians 2:9). And this promise is *not* limited to the afterlife! God's promise starts *now* as God heals our hearts.

This healing process involves each of us in relationship to others: other people, the human community, the world, the whole of creation. When Jesus affirmed the expert in the Law (Luke 10:27–28) who summarized the commandments of God as "You must love the Most High God with all your heart, with all your soul, with all your strength, and with all your mind, and your neighbor as yourself," Jesus was reminding us that *love of self, love of every other person, and love of God* are interrelated. We cannot love one adequately without loving the others. As we ourselves experience healing, our newfound liberation and well-being and self-worth enable us to reach out with compassion to others and the world. We experience kinship with every created being, much in the way St. Francis of Assisi did.

Our ability to reach out to others arises from our gratitude to the intimately caring God whom we are experiencing as our healer and the healer of all. As we become aware of the ongoing action of God in our own hearts and in others' lives and in the whole of creation, we feel bound to one another and to God in the dynamic dance that is Trinitarian Love. And in this dance we are "holding hands," or "holding hearts." This is the basis of intercession.

This kind of prayer is a powerhouse because we go to the vision in the mind and heart of God and pray in it. That is what it means "to pray in Jesus' name." "In Jesus' name," in the understanding of the Hebrew of his day, meant, "in Jesus' very person"! And the person of Jesus is *one* with Abba-God in everything. As Jesus taught us, "whatever you ask of Abba God in my name God will give you. This command I give you: that you love one another" (John 15:16–17). He was emphatic in this teaching: "Love one another *as I have loved you*" (15:12, emphasis added).

We must not put off until tomorrow the good we can do for ourselves, for others, and for the world today. We need to begin *now* to pray in affirmation-style so that the prayer-wish of Jesus, at least in the little world that surrounds each of us, may be fulfilled: "that my joy may be yours, and your joy may be complete" (John 15:11).

About the Authors

Bridget Mary Meehan, a Sister for Christian Community (SFCC), holds a doctorate in ministry from Virginia Theological Seminary. She is a spiritual director, conference speaker, consultant in women's spirituality, and author of fifteen books, including *The Healing Power of Prayer* (Liguori Publications, 1996), *God Delights in You, Prayers and Activities for Catholic Families, Exploring the Feminine Face of God, Delighting in the Feminine Divine,* and *Heart Talks with Mother God.* Dr. Meehan offers a visionary approach to wholeness and healing for women and men as disciples of Jesus and equals in the contemporary world. She is a producer and host of *Godtalk,* a new cable TV program that aims to nurture the soul, heal the heart, expand consciousness, transform lives, and inspire believers of all faiths.

Regina Madonna Oliver, a Sister for Christian Community (SFCC), is also known by her given name of Loris Lee Oliver. She holds an M.A. from Marquette University, an M.T.S. from the Washington Theological Union, and a D.Min. from the Graduate Theological Foundation, Donaldson, Indiana. An educator at all levels from kindergarten through high school, she spent the last fourteen years in pastoral ministry in a military chapel, where she was active in liturgical ministry, hospital ministry, and adult spiritual programs. With Bridget Mary Meehan she co-authored *Heart Talks with Mother God.*